A Journey Back to Self

Self

---

101 Meditations & Quotes for

Awakening Your Buddha Nature

Tiger Dragon Storm

Published in 2017 by Heartspace House
Publishing

ISBN-13:
978-1999767709
ISBN-10:
1999767705

Preface

This book began as notes from a human being unknowingly on a spiritual journey to finding *truth*. What is *God*? What are *Emotions?* What's the purpose of *Life*? Can these questions be answered by a seemingly normal person?

It's only now that I've realised I've been on a spiritual path for a long time, well, everything is spiritual when you look underneath the curtain of ego. I've been having other-worldly experiences since I was a child, experiences that at the time I didn't know were extra-ordinary, but have since realised in my latter years they were indeed "Other" in human understanding.

From an enormous golden bird of light that I used to call an "Eagle", regularly appearing before me as I went to sleep. To talking to myself with the awareness that there's a listener to the talking within me…so…who was the *real* me I questioned. To more recently, having an experience of walking above my head. As I walked down the street, my vision split into two places, through my physical eyes and above my head simultaneously. I could see around corners with this ability, I knew exactly which number bus was coming around the corner before my physical eyes saw it. Sounds strange I know! But hey, life is indeed a mystery and I'm sure you the reader have some interesting experiences you could share with me if we ever meet in our physical forms.

Through self-enquiry and meditation, my questions and answers on what this entity we call *Life* came. Life is an exciting journey that is a mystery to be solved and explored, and not a problem to be fixed. I wish you a pleasant read exploring the deepest parts of your mind's spiritual basement.

How to Read

This Book

Dear reader, here are 3 Important things I'd like you to know before you read this book:

1) What is meditation? Meditation is the act of seeking a meditative state. To be in a meditative state is to be fully present in the moment. This happens often throughout our day without our realising. When you wash the dishes, completely focused on a tough dirty spot that needs extra attention, you're only aware of that spot, so, this spot becomes your whole universe. This is a basic form of the meditative state.

2) This book can be read from front to back if you so wish. But, life has shown me in ways that I cannot ignore, the questions we didn't know we had, and the answers that we seek, always come to us when we need them the most.

I recommend that you use this book in the way a Tarot Reader would ask you to pick a random card from her or his deck, the card revealing what you need to know, in the present time.

Please pick your pages at random (though you'll soon realise nothing is random) for a more exciting way to use this book. Also, this will enhance your intuition's ability in the process. As you'll rely on feeling and energy more than the ego.

3) Meditation. This book's format entails a quote, underneath the quote a "Meditation". The quotes are a mixture of easy to follow, to extremely thought-provoking lessons. This is to ensure no matter how far along you feel your journey of seeking truth is, you'll be learning something valuable to help you achieve your goals. Do not assume you must be great at meditating in the picturesque sense of eyes closed cross-legged in a perfect lotus position whilst executing aum chants for hours at a time. Though you may choose that method of course if it's your most comfortable way of meditating.

For what I'm asking you to do, any meditation novice can do.

After you've read the respective meditation to the quote, put the book down, and just stop…just…stop. Sit down, or lie down. Take a few deep breaths in through your nose, exhaling out of your mouth. Breathing consciously, helps to bring one's focus to un-focusing on what may come (which creates potential for anxiety to arise) and brings them back to the here and now. Next, either think of the quote through the act of contemplation to find its meaning(s), or focus on the space in between your thoughts to perceive the words and feelings which arise. There is an energy in *truth* that is always felt by us, it's that innate knowing that resonates within. Because you are that truth. The *Meditation* underneath the quote, is there to give you some pointers, a head start, on which mental lane to travel down with (or without) your mind

Some of the meditations will have the answer within its words, some will have several questions for you to ponder that will take you to an answer that feels pure of heart.

The most important thing for you to do in your meditations is to be present in the *now,* for now is all you have, feel it, be here and through this you will discover how to meditate deeply.

For meditation is simply about being in the present moment.

By doing this act alone, your consciousness will expand as your limiting ego with all its belief systems that you attach to, will not affect *you*.

These quotes and meditations will help you in your day to day life, in your search for consciousness expansion, and if you do the meditations thoroughly, you will find true Self. All of this is possible, use this book to help you remember that which you are.

Now,

Let Us

Begin...

1 "Self-realisation is the

most important

realisation needing to be

realised"

Meditation: it's not about "who", for the "who" is a man-made concept, a so-called "person", but "what" are you? Meditate on this *what*. Always remembering that the person you think you are is only what you've been told. There's a part of you that still exist whether thoughts, emotions or actions are happening within you or not, thus they cannot be who *you* are. This awareness must be looked at. Ask you yourself, can the one who watches your thoughts, be seen also? Who is thinking? Who is watching the thinking? Where do *you* come into all of this?

2 "You've already lived a million lives, make this your best one yet"

Meditation: Do you believe in *past* lives? If not, how can you confirm you're not living in your *past* life right now?

3 "Darkness is the canvas on which light paints upon"

Meditation: Duality exist in everything from the perspective of the finite mind, meet the side of yourself you've denied existed and make friends with that self. If you've been aware of that side for some time, love that side even more for it is a part of your many forms. Do not deny it, love it for making it possible for your light to shine. From the perspective of the infinite consciousness that you truly are, duality does not exist, for everything is happening at the same time. Realising the Self, is to realise the individual person does not exist, separation is an illusion that our individual mind creates. You're no-thing, and everything, you're dark, and light, for all is an expression of consciousness. Do not rush the second understanding that all is one, this is the enlightenment one reaches through breaking off parts of their attachment to their person bit by bit. Then one day, the ego personality will seem like a character in a movie and the whole world will be perceived as it really is, many variations of the one consciousness.

4 "No-thing exist without a space to hold it in, and an awareness of its presence. Just as your personality needs a body to express itself, existence in all its glory could not exist without a space to exist within or an

awareness of its

existence"

Meditation: Marinate in the feeling of space being the 5th element, understand how important it is. For even *God* of the religious understanding needs space to exist, so which came first? What you call God/Universe or the space to allow for it to exist. If it is the space, was this space created? Or is it something that is always there? Plus, the knowledge of God/Universe would have to come from a consciousness outside of it, could it be that

consciousness is eternal and all arise from
it? Is Consciousness what *God* really is?

5 "Pain arrives when harmony leaves"

Meditation: Pain is caused by a resistance to something, what are you resisting right now?

6 "Your life is a story, you're not the subject you're the author"

Meditation: There is a part of you that is unaffected by this perceived physical world, it has time to observe all those thoughts you are having and watch those images in your imagination, who is that one?

7 "Thoughts don't make you unhappy, attaching to thoughts make you unhappy"

Meditation: One reason for your stress or depression, is due to your attachment to thought. Which is the attachment to the idea that you are the person thinking the thoughts. Which cannot be true since you do not know the next thought you will perceive. You only suffer through the belief that you *are* the thought, instead of you being the *witness* to the thought. No thought or feeling is stronger than your intention, for intention is the part of you who decides, who chooses what will affect this body in this life. It's not the thoughts, thoughts are only allowed to affect you with your permission. No, it isn't easy to reduce one's attention to thought, but with practice this ability becomes extremely plausible. So, start right now. Meditate on the knowing that a thought is not the boss of you, you are the boss of it. See how it feels when you give attention to a thought verses less and less attention to a thought.

8 "Don't marry a

negative thought"

Meditation: The more you commit to a
negative thought the more it lives with you.
Don't marry the thought, let go of it and
move on. In addition to this, understand
that negative thoughts are only negative if
you perceive them that way. Seeing a
thought as "negative", only increases
resistance in you making you feel unhappy
that you have them. Instead of attaching
labels such as "positive" or "negative" to

them, see thought for what it is...thought. Don't judge the thought, just sit back and observe from a distance in your meditation.

9 "Each forgiveness creates a new beginning"

Meditation: You must forgive before you can move on, the purest sense of you knows this, but your ego won't accept that an era in your life is over, or won't accept what somebody did to you. Meditate on who or what in your life has angered/troubled you and forgive yourself for being in that situation. for when we forgive, we exit the victimhood mind state and reclaim our much-needed power and self-esteem.

10 "The sun is always shining

even when it rains, your

light still exists even in

moments of pain"

Meditation: Right now, you need to become like the sun, strong, always unaffected by Earthly matters, and knows who it *really* is no matter what is done with its light rays on Earth. Remember your life here on Earth is but a fraction of not who, but what you are.

Become the sun.

11 "Death. You don't
grow old then die, you
grow into that which you
were before you synced
with the body you
believe that you are, that
which you were before
you latched on to the
identity your parents

gave you when they

(re)named you with an

earthly name, you drop

all identity and become

that which you truly are

you become ageless,

formless, pure

intelligence yet pure

emptiness, you become

pure awareness"

Meditation: You're made of the universe, thus you're as *old* as the universe. The universe itself could not exist without an awareness behind it confirming its existence of which must be…you…meditate on this powerful message.

12 "When we rush, we cause ourselves bad health, for when we rush, we are stressed"

Meditation: Rushing is always due to a lack of preparation for your day. Of course, there are things that can happen suddenly during our day, that we absolutely need to rush for. But this meditation is about the countless preventable situations like being late for work, meetings, getting the kids to school, buying your partner that birthday card etc. These are all preventable and can be turned into rush-less endeavors with the correct planning of your day, which should firstly involve waking up earlier to prepare for the day ahead. If you find it difficult to wake up earlier than you usually do, look at your diet and the time you go to bed at night, for those two things could be the reason you wake up feeling groggy and needing that extra five mins' snooze. Also, meditate on what things you could change in your life to create more time in your day. Even if you manage to create one extra minute, it shows you it's possible, therefore making it easier for you to create an extra 2 mins,3 mins and so on in your day. Do this and reduce stress in your life.

13 "If they cannot see their plight, you must be their sight"

Meditation: We often believe something to be true or good for us that turns out really isn't. From that ex-partner being "the one" to bad business investments. We can be blinded by emotion as to what's right for us. Our friends/family may give us their opinion on whatever it is we feel we want, and we sometimes disregard their words because we feel we know best. The thing is, if they are not emotional about what you are wanting, they will have a better clarity of vision in what you are wanting. Plus vice versa, you see what your friends/family don't see when they are reacting to the emotional feeling of what they want that you know will be wrong for them, which in turn prompts you to offer your opinion from your less emotional perspective which will be clearer. Meditate on the understanding that not only must we give advice, we must conversely be open to receiving advice.

14 "The population of your world is 1...just you"

Meditation: There is the world we all share called Earth. But, there are also psychological worlds which are individual to us. In these worlds, our unique preferences and perceptions keep us as individual entities. Meditate on the knowing that no two people are ever *exactly the same*, therefore, you are the Master of your universe for you are unlike anybody in all of

existence

15 "Decide what gets your physical attention"

Meditation: You must learn to conserve your energy as energy is what you are. Decide who or what gets your physical, emotional and mental energy. Not everything that enters your awareness needs a reaction from you, for the more energy you give out the less you'll keep for yourself.

16 "The true meaning of the words *I love you,* is I love the part of you that exist within me"

Meditation: We reflect each other's
emotions like mirrors reflect our physicality.
Love must first arise within us before we
can offer it to somebody else. Thus, love, is
a co-creation of a beautiful experience.
Bathe yourself in the fragrance of
understanding that love, is always shared
in one way or another

43

17 "What you like/dislike in me, is what you like/dislike about yourself"

Meditation: We reflect one another like mirrors. What you dislike or like in somebody is the energy they are creating in you due to your reaction to how they are. Be at ease with emotion, and know that you're not the emotion itself.

18 "Consciousness does not need a brain, but the brain needs consciousness"

Meditation: Consciousness can't originate from the brain, for the awareness of the brain's existence must come first. The brain does not know it's a brain. But consciousness, and you are consciousness, confirms it is a brain. So, consciousness *must* be outside the brain to confirm that which it perceives. All is an expression of consciousness including the brain, consciousness must come before any object to confirm the object's existence. Does it make sense to you that the brain can consciously create consciousness without the consciousness already in existence? Or does the notion that all is an expression of consciousness make more sense?

19 "Everybody is vibrating at their own unique frequency of consciousness, so speak your truth, if their ego allows it they'll match your frequency and join your wavelength of consciousness and

48

understanding, if not, who cares? That's their business not yours"

Meditation: Be Conscious of how much energy you spend explaining yourself, don't overdo it. For if somebody is in a state of resistance, and you try to reason with them, they won't see the reason no matter how hard you try. Your carrying on will only enter you into a competition of egos. Meditate on situations you've had like this, and see how they would have panned out if you simply said your truth and let it be

instead of pushing for them to *get* you.

20 "Melt into the moment"

Meditation: The moment is all you have, so don't waste time thinking of another one for the future is an illusion, *now* is the only real thing you have

21 "You're alive!

Appreciate that"

Meditation: Appreciation begets inner peace. Start appreciating the fact you're alive more often. For the meaning of life...is life.

22 "You're not just flesh, you're a magnet, everything you think, feel, or say, will be attracted into your awareness"

Meditation: Think of yourself as an energetic magnet for that is the reality of what you are. You attract what you think feel or say into your awareness

23 "Own your mind, stay above it, don't *be* it"

Meditation: Don't let your mind control you, for you're greater than it. Don't let the mind stress you out, for you're greater than it. You're the awareness that exist so it can't harm you with negative thoughts unless you believe you are the mind. Meditate on this question, are *you* the mind? or something other than it?

24 "No trouble exist that will not become a distant memory"

Meditation: The troubles you perceive yourself as having cannot last forever, they will pass. Think of your worries as entities being carried by trains, and your mind as the station. The trains carrying your worries will not last at your station for long, you know they will pass by you eventually, moving on into the un-seeable distance.

Now, know your perceived troubles will also pass

25 "Don't let your tool that humanity has named *ego* distract you from your purpose...the purpose of experiencing this physical life"

Meditation: Your fears are carried by your ego, don't allow it to stop you from experiencing the wonders of this world.

26 "You're that, which you've been searching for"

Meditation: You *are* that truth that you seek. Look behind the mind to find it. For *something* is there that never leaves. *Something* greater than the mind itself. The journey to your truth requires no distance, no boat, bike or car. For you're looking from the place of the truth you're searching for.

27 "How to manifest your desires through the Law of attraction.

Think of desire (attention)

Stop thinking of desire (released resistance)

Match the emotion of receiving the desire (frequency match)"

Meditation: Follow the order in the quote above, on how to manifest your desires, and see how well you can make it work for you in this physical reality.

28 "Crying when sad releases negative energy making way for new energy to arise and blossom from within"

Meditation: Our tears are necessary for several functions, one of those important functions is for the transportation of overwhelming energy. The body can only hold onto so much energy at any given time, so whether you are crying of laughter or from sadness, our tears kick into gear to release excess energy for our bodies to stay as healthy as possible. Do you ever hold your tears back? If so, how did it make you feel? Why are you afraid to show this level of emotion which is completely healthy and normal? Go now, travel inwards, to meet the person inside you and ask him/her if any energy needs to be released right now in the form of tears. You will feel all the better for the release if it is needed.

29 "You'll stop attracting that which you don't prefer once you've healed the part of yourself that still needs it"

Meditation: The same way they say you can't run from your problems, is the same way you can't cover up the parts of you that still needs healing. We live in our vibrational bodies in a vibrational universe, things can only exist if we are on a similar wavelength to them. Whether people or objects. Cats can see frequencies of light that we cannot, because we are not able to perceive that vibrational range. Your emotional problems are vibrational thought forms that hang around you until you stop ignoring them and deal with them. Reality has a way to force us to deal with that which we ignore. Thus, forcing us to take notice. Our trigger could be us getting sick, losing a relationship a car a job etc. Healing is a huge part of life that evades no person on Earth. What you must do now is go inwards via meditation to look at that thought that triggers you and accept that it does, then look for the root of the problem. This may take a while, take as long as you need, minutes, days, months, years

whatever it takes to heal yourself. The most

important thing is you start the healing

process.

30 "Unapologetically me"

Meditation: Life is too short to not live in your authentic truth, you will not be in this lifetime forever. So, start living it as the real *you* that *you* know *you* are. Meditate on who the real *you* in this lifetime wishes to be, then strive towards achieving it.

31 "Pay attention to your intention"

Meditation: Your intention charges up your desires like a battery. The clearer the intention the quicker that which you want manifested whether good or bad will be realised. Pay attention to what your intentions are in this situation.

32 "Your thoughts create your world"

Meditation: You hold the *power* of intention within you, thoughts, which are forms of energy will always come, it's down to *your* attention to the thought that will result in the outcome of how your world shapes up.

Energy flows where attention goes, therefore your thoughts create your world

33 "Complete free will is

an illusion for all action

is reaction"

Meditation: This understanding is not for the faint hearted, but something inside of you has been drawn to read this quote and its meditation as part of you is seeking a larger truth. You are challenged right here and now, to do something, absolutely anything, that was not influenced by the

69

outside or your *inner* world. This includes
not being influenced by anything from:

Thought

The elements

People

Your Body etc.

You will soon come to see that everything
you do is a reaction to the previous
moment and that *all action is a reaction.*
Meditate on this, feel how much free-will
you have in life. If any at all.

34 Stress is %100 based on how you react to a situation"

Meditation: It's all about where your focus is, are you focusing in a way that says, "This is too much!" "I can't do this!". Or, is your focus saying "Ok, how can I adapt to this situation?" "How can I work this out". Think of the last stressful situation you had, and really feel if it had to result in your stress levels rising, or if you could have reacted differently to help your stress level stay normal.

35 "Many arguments are caused simply from your tone of voice"

Meditation: Just like the jarring sound of a hammer on a wall or the screeching sound that can be made on a blackboard, we get triggered into a state of annoyance. The frequency of your voice itself can jar people into a triggered state also, thus causing arguments and even fights. So be wary of your vocal delivery in communicating your thoughts, don't be overly conscious of your

tone, but be aware...as it could prevent a
misunderstanding which could lead to an
unnecessary argument. Meditate on this
knowing, for it will help you stay calm in
your next interaction with a person who's
tone of voice is dissonant to your current
state of being.

36 "Absolute nothing simply cannot exist. It's a religious concept that takes power away from your eternal self. For even when one says *nothing* one has inadvertently conceptualised the

nothing into something,

and now this *nothing*

itself, has an awareness

observing that the so-

called *nothing* is

there...therefore...that

awareness...must be

you"

Meditation: What is nothing? Does absolute nothing exist? Or is it simply a philosophical concept? Search for this space of nothingness in your meditative state and see what you find.

37 "You never lose, you just learn a new lesson"

Meditation: Life is about learning through experience. You only "lose" if your perception of losing equals "loss". In one sense, you may have technically "lost" a football match or the promotion at work to the other person but it can be perceived as gain also. There are two sides to everything, so instead of saying "I lost", you can say "I'm gaining experience in how to better myself to be the best version of me. Now, explore through meditation the dualities you see in life from the finite

mind's perspective and bask in its beauty,

for nothing is what it seems.

38 "The wise know nothing"

Meditation: At the exact moment, you admit to yourself that you don't know something, the chance to grow in knowledge and wisdom will begin to flower within you.

39 "Regularly seeing synchronistic numbers is a sign that your life is in order"

Meditation: Synchronistic numbers such as seeing 00:00 on a clock or noticing your football team scored the winning goal in the 55th minute of the match with the number

55 jersey on the scorers back, show you that your life is trying to tell you something. Different numbers hold different frequencies therefore have different messages about specific parts of your life that is in order. I've created a short numerology description to help you understand what the numbers mean. Although of course, they may mean something different to you, the below descriptions are the basics of what numbers 0-9, 11 and 22 means in western numerology.

Numbers of numerology short descriptions both *positive* and *negative*:

0 - Boundless possibility, the true self, stuck in your ways, boring.

1 – Success, leadership, loneliness, self-absorbed

2 – Love, empathy, Shyness, neediness.

3 – Playfulness, creative, immature, too easy going

4 – Reliable, hard-working, unimaginative, too serious.

5- Adventurous, free thinker, lack of discipline, un-reliable.

6 – Joyful, helpful, moody, gossiper.

7 – Wisdom, spiritual, skeptical, arrogant.

8 – Powerful persona, financially abundant, greedy, untrustworthy.

9 – Great mentor, pushes the limits of the norm, vain, too extreme.

11 – Psychic, visionary, un-grounded in reality, feelings of superiority/inferiority.

22 – Enlightened, compassionate, stubborn, intense rage

Now meditate with the intention to be shown numbers or a number, don't force the number to reveal itself. The number(s) that comes into your awareness is the number that is trying to tell you something you need to know right now. If you see a number that is not on the list, simply add the numbers individually until you get a number on the list. for example;

654 = 6 +5+4 =15 1 +5 = 6

Number 6 would be the number in this example that is mirroring your current vibration.

40 "Don't be too quick to judge another person for everybody has been through some pain, and theirs may be greater than your own"

Meditation: We carry hurts from this life and other lives happening in other realms. Trying to cover up or forget our pains only serves to keep them hanging around gaining more momentum to hurt you over and over until you learn your lesson. Seek help if you feel hurt right now, whether from another person or through meditation. We must do this to cause the weight of hurt to lift off of us like a butterfly off a flower.

41 "If you can be more silent than silence, your higher self will communicate to you in the form of inspiration"

Meditation: Only in the silence can we raise our vibration to match our pure self. To perceive/feel our purest self, be silent, or chant a high vibration mantra like AUM to help you focus. As AUM is a universal sound. Meditate and observe the silence, either do this silently or observe the space between your chants. *Raising our vibration in the sense that we remove our egos to be as pure as our highest self.*

42 "Next time you think of buying something you don't need, first ask yourself, how much food can this money buy for this week"

Meditation: To buy on impulse is to be a compulsive and reactive person, this is not a person in control of themselves. To have balance and peace in one's life, one must be more proactive instead of reacting to what the ego is telling one to buy. Debt is one of the leading causes of stress in our so-called modern society, partly caused by how the banking system works. But can you turn the focus towards yourself and be honest and see that sometimes you are buying things you don't *need* but instead *want*? Even when you know you will plunge into or further into debt if you do? Have a look at your life, see if you are a reactive consumer or a proactive one.

43 "We are always expanding, are you expanding into fear? Or love?"

Meditation: Each thought and belief you have creates a new path for you to journey down. You may have noticed throughout your life that once you became aware of something whether it was an object, idea, event or person, that it showed up in your awareness more and more. You create your world with that which you give

attention to. That which you give attention

to is thought. So where is your attention

right now...is it expanding you into fear? or

love?

44 "Giving in to anger and fear will not stop you from dying, but it will stop you from living."

Meditation: This doesn't mean ignore your feelings, it just means make peace with them or they will change you into somebody you do not wish to be.

45 "It isn't the drink or smoke that you need, it's self-esteem and always has been, those substances are just a convenient distraction from facing up to a part of yourself that needs looking at...healing. Just

like all compulsions,

compulsive behavior is

allowing something

outside of oneself to

control them"

Meditation: Substances such as alcohol,

cigarettes, processed sugar and caffeine,

are addictive drugs that alters your body to

manipulate your emotion(s). Relying on an

item to keep you balanced is no sign of

mental freedom. Unless you have a chronic

disease, finding the root cause of your addiction is the first step to regaining your mental and emotion freedom. Do you wish to feel free within your body? Meditate on the *whys* of why you are so dependent on certain emotional altering substances if you currently are. Identifying the memory, and emotion of what you're trying to cover up, is the first and most important step to healing.

46 "Your current situation is always your most important situation, for your future relies on it"

Meditation: Looking too far ahead causes unnecessary anxiety, take one moment at a time, one step at a time. I challenge you to present 1 second of the future to your friends, can this be done? or is the future non-existent?

47 "I don't live years, I live moments"

Meditation: A year cannot be experienced in its entirety, you only can experience the moment. So, what is time really?

48 "Truth is thicker than lies"

Meditation: Truth will always out-weigh a lie. Look at your life, can you confirm this by using your life as an example? Has a lie you've told or that has been said to you, been revealed as a lie at some point after it was said?

49 "Do not draw conclusions on who you think you are"

Meditation: From this moment till the next you're essentially a different person, as no matter how small it may be, the person you're in the next moment will have more life experience than the previous one. Have you drawn a conclusion on who you knew you were, that later changed into somebody with new beliefs, likes and dislikes? Meditate on this knowing that

you're ever-changing and it's this
understanding that keeps things new in
your life and keeps you hopeful in times of
adversity.

50 "Be consciously ignorant"

Meditation: Become consciously ignorant, stay open, but conscious. For as soon as we say we "know" we create a barrier of bias that prevents us from learning and accepting new information, from accepting *truth*.

51 "Consciousness is free and you are consciousness"

Meditation: The human consciousness is like a bird in a cage without a door.

Through patient but thorough self-enquiry, enquiring who the perceiver of our thoughts is, we become more consciously aware, we experience the fact that...there is no cage and never has been. Do this powerful, and timeless, self-enquiry now and forever have your perception on who you are changed.

52 "Truth doesn't care how you feel"

Meditation: Sometimes the truth hurts, but it will always remain what it is...*truth.*

53 "Truth is the highest form of love"

Meditation: Truth holds no resistance, truth is the purest thing that can exist. Honor your truth and other's truths. Truth is a blessing and doesn't reveal itself to everyone all the time. Appreciate *truth*, for it is a virtue.

54 "Peace over ego"

Meditation: The moment you realise you can't please everyone, is the moment you realise you don't have to please everyone, with this realisation you'll discover peace of mind

55 "I am not the body"

Meditation: Relax, and observe the expansion and contraction of your torso. Since this process happens without your say so, does this make it clear enough to you that you are not the body? Look at your hand, and make it quadruple in size...can you do this? Why not? If you are it, the body, then you should be able to do what you like. Why is there a limit to what you can do if you *are* the body? the same way you drive a car and know you are not the car itself, is the same way you are not the body. Last thing you can try right now to

determine if you are the body or not, is to
hold your breath and count to 10 in your
mind, then exhale. Did the voice that did
the counting, struggle to speak, as the body
was cut off from oxygen? If the voice that
tells you, you are you, does not need
oxygen, and is unaffected by what happens
to this body...then could it be...*you* are
elsewhere controlling this body from afar?
Meditate on this life changing subject.

56 "Your body belongs to Earth, but you don't"

Meditation: What makes you, *you* is your personality. Your personality is not your body. So, where are you? The part of you that thinks? Who is thinking? Who is deciding which thoughts are to be created? Meditate on where you truly are. Do you even have a location? Enjoy this powerful self-enquiry.

57 "Appreciation can choose to reveal itself in the form of hating"

Meditation: Hating, is often the jealousy or admiration for what you're achieving in your life. If you sense somebody's hate being directed towards you right now, just know they could well be masking their appreciation for who you are and what you are doing. Things are not always as they seem, look deeper into why someone may be hating you right now. Can you relate this to your own life? Have you dished out this irrational hating before? Look at why that was and confirm if it was indeed your jealousy or admiration in disguise. From now on, be more consciously aware of the duality of emotion.

58 "One must innerstand before one can understand"

Meditation: Too many people fail to realise the power of happiness comes from our own *choice* to feel happy, hurt or sad. It all stems from within, it's all about *how* we react to situations that life matches us up with, understanding this takes you to a deeper level of *innerstanding.*

59 "Appreciation of nature is a key ingredient to achieving peace of mind"

Meditation: You're nature, and nature is you. Knowing this, would you say you're more important than a tree? Less? Or the same?

60 "People want to be healthy, but don't want to live healthy"

Meditation: Do you have a desire to be healthy right now? Does this desire match up with your actions?

61 "The mind can never be set"

Meditation: You can become a different person a new you anytime you choose. How? It all depends on which thoughts you choose to believe in. How much does this notion resonate with you? Does life change according to your beliefs? Or are your beliefs dependent on what life presents you? Use your life as an example.

62 "Intention is the sword that cuts the strings of your desires"

Meditation: Think of your life, have you always held a strong enough intention to the desire you sought that never came to be? What about your current life desires, is your intention for them as clear as the blue sky on a Summer's day? Or cloudy like an Autumn evening? Only through clear intention will your desires receive enough energy to manifest into your world. You need to be able to visualise what you want without attaching to distracting thoughts. The "ifs" and "buts" in your life are the clouds that block the clarity of your sky-blue intention.

63 "Stop thinking, start knowing"

Meditation: Reclaim your individual power, we are all born with power. Instead of believing what people, the news and books tell you, seek the truth for yourself. Stay in a place of 99% believing until you know. Only then can you be 100% about anything. What have you been so sure about in your life, maybe a *fact* you were told at school, that later was debunked? Stay open until you know, instead of only believing.

64 "We have three eyes, two for looking and another to see"

Meditation: Your body has an inner sight known by many people in spiritual communities around the world as the *third eye*. This *eye*, has the clarity to see beyond physical, mental and emotional illusions. It deals with the more subtler energies. To help you develop this *inner-sight*, meditate with your eyes closed, and place your focus slightly upwards in line with your eyebrows to look through this eye. Keep bringing your focus back to that spot if it wavers. What do you see or feel when focusing in this area of your body? As real as this ability your body possesses is, the deeper question now arises, what is perceiving the *third eye* to confirm its existence? Could it be a fourth eye?

65 "Positivity is not so positive"

Meditation: The popular new age western philosophy of *positive thinking* to change a situation, is in effect *forcing* positivity to exist. Forcing positivity does not defeat negativity. It only creates more resistance within yourself. When we resist something, we give that something equal attention. Thus, forcing positivity does not negate the negativity at all. It's better to allow and deal with the situation at hand, as it is, with complete clarity and no illusions.

66 "The world smiles when you smile"

Meditation: Understand, that you're extremely important to this world, for when you smile, the whole world increases its happiness by 1

67 "We're all connected, when you hurt someone else you hurt yourself too"

Meditation: Empathy is our ability to feel another's emotional state. Proving that we are all connected on an energetic level. To intend on hurting somebody, the feeling of hurt must first arise within you to guide you into committing the action. Thus, you will *feel* the hurt you inflict. Meditate on more peaceful ways to solve conflict that may appear in your life.

68 "When you realise your true self, it becomes impossible to ever feel alone again"

Meditation: For you to *have* a *Self*, you must not be the *Self*, itself. What does this mean?

69 "There is no past or future they do not exist, therefore, now is your whole life"

Meditation: Can you live in any moment but the present? If not, you agree every perceived moment is the same moment and the only one ever in existence. The following question then arises, how can you confirm you were ever born?

70 "I am my best friend"

Meditation: Yourself is the one who never leaves you. So, it makes perfect sense to make friends with that which is your being, your essence. Does your-self have a physicality? A sound? Now meet your-self/soul/spirit whatever you call the one that speaks to you through the channel of your mind. Do you need to travel to meet this one? Do you need to take a plane or car to meet this one?

71 "I am the King of my reality"

Meditation: Know that you're the King/Queen of your reality, as it is yours after all. Nobody can live your life and have your exact perspective other than you. Never forget your life is yours and yours only to live.

72 "Nature heals my nature"

Meditation: Nothing teaches us how to just be...like nature does. Go out into nature and observe its willingness to be exactly what it is with no confusions within its essence. Be like nature, for nature is you.

73 "Atheists and theists are essentially on the same page, for neither of them know experientially if a God/Creator exists or not"

Meditation: Before looking for God, one must first know that which they are. What is left of you when you do not think, use emotion or words, but just stay still and silent? Find out now, sit in the place between your thoughts, be still and silent. What do you find in this space? Does this sense of you have physicality? Could it get sick? Does it have desires? Could it die? Where does thought arise from? If one does not yet know where thought arises from, the same thoughts that tell you who you are, why worry about God being real or not, when you don't even know what *you* are? Could it be that you are G...?

74 "Attachment to a negative thought is the root of all unhappiness"

Meditation: You do not need to allow unhappy thoughts to bring you down to its level. Begin to separate yourself from thought. For you are separate from it. Thought will always exist, but it is not you, for if it were, you would know exactly what your next thought would be. But you do not, you only become aware of the thought when it is in front of you. Where is this thought when you are not focused on it?

Can it be created from absolute nothing?

Who is the one who decides whether or not

a thought gets its attention? Go inwards.

75 "Happiness owes you nothing"

Meditation: Chasing an emotion is like chasing the wind, for all emotions come and go, happiness is no exception to that rule. Don't chase the feeling of being happy, learn to be at peace in that place between each passing emotion. Take a deep inhale, then exhale, then focus on that short space in between the next inhale. Focus on the breath as this will help you detach from thought. Focus on that small but powerful gap, for this will help you get to a no-mind state which is the understanding that you exist beyond mind and therefore all thought. Who is there in this place? What is there? Are you unhappy in this place? Or Completely unaffected by emotion? This space is the true meditative state.

76 "Overthinking suffocates your mental freedom"

Meditation: The more you repeat the same thought, the more familiar with it you become, the more familiar with it you become, the harder it is to leave its side. Overthinking stops you from allowing new fresh energy into yourself. Overcome overthinking by learning to trust your innate knowing that you are born with. Using your life as an example, how often have you said to yourself "I knew I should have done that"? when we don't trust ourselves and overthink situations, we make things more complex than they are. Generally, your initial feeling is the correct one. How true is this to you?

77 "You're more *everything* than you think"

Meditation: What you truly are, the truth
that you seek, cannot be intellectualised.
Because the mental capacity we have is
simply a tool to use that enables us to track
our growth in the physical egoic world. So,
when you think you are strong, you are
truly stronger, when you think you're happy,
you're happier even than that. Go beyond

mind, for mind is your tool to use but isn't

you.

78 "Attaching to negativity is not your responsibility"

Meditation: I am responsible for my happiness and sadness through my attention to what does or does not serve my joy. I realise I am neither happiness nor sadness but the observer of the two.

79 "You're not conscious, you're consciousness"

Meditation: To say, "I am conscious", implies you are a self-aware being. But what observes this being you believe you are that states he/she is conscious? Have you ever been aware of a time when you were not conscious? To be aware of not being conscious is still consciousness being aware of its apparent lack of consciousness. You are consciousness itself, you birth other forms of consciousness humanity has named *ego*, personality, but what *you* are must be the eternal consciousness as you are always aware of something or at least aware of your awareness. Can you ever know you're not conscious? if not, how can you confirm you've ever *not* been conscious or aware in some way?

80 "If you say you don't have enough time, then you won't have enough time, if you say you do have enough time, you'll create enough time"

Meditation: How can you say you don't have enough time, when time isn't anything more than an agreed upon construct? It isn't a natural phenomenon, as past and future only exist in individual minds. So, is it this so-called *time* you don't have? Or are you blaming your circumstance on an imaginary entity?

81 "Love your mistakes, for they are your tough-love guides that keep you conscious of your unconscious actions"

Meditation: Your perceived mistakes are not negative, they're reminders and lessons that stay with you more strongly than any book could offer you. You will keep making them until you understand the ultimate message of your perceived mistakes, no matter how great or small, is to be consciously aware in your moment, being too fast with your thoughts or actions can result in what we've labeled as mistakes.

82 "When you live in your heart, good things happen to you"

Meditation: We experience pain when we live in a vibration of fear. Living in the heart space is living in a non-resistant allowing space, allowing creates ease, ease creates less stress, less stress equals a happier person.

83 "The more you have to explain yourself, the guiltier you sound"

Meditation: Think of times in your life when you've known somebody was lying to your face. How did you know they were lying? What was it about their explanation?

84 "Strong people know how to show compassion in a hard world"

Meditation: Strength is shown in many ways. Meditate on the importance of being the loving compassionate person people can take example of. Do you wish to be a person who perpetuates the notion that *life is hard*? Or do you wish to change this notion and breathe a new compassionate life into humanity?

85 "Each time you say the words *I want*, you stray further away from that which you seek"

Meditation: You're more than I as I equals ego, ego is something you have, not that which you are. Your wanting of something perpetuates the feeling within you, that you

don't have the that which you want, further

extending the distance between you and

that which you desire. Be conscious with

your words, as words can become self-

fulfilling prophecies. Subtract the ego and

desire, and you will be left holding that

which you seek.

86 "My body and mind need me"

Meditation: If you can find time to care enough to recharge your phone battery, you can find time and care enough to recharge your body and mind.

87 "Memories are both a blessing and a curse"

Meditation: The ability to remember is a gift that can be used for our growth or decline. The more we dwell on memories we label as *bad* memories, the worse we feel, the more we take inspiration from *good* memories the better we feel. Learn to *use* memory, don't let it use you. View memory just as it is, a moment that has *past* that cannot harm you whether you perceive it as a good or bad memory.

88 "The more security we seek, the less secure we reveal ourselves to be"

Meditation: We need physical security in our lives, but too much of anything causes unbalance. The more emotional security you seek, like protecting ourselves from rejection, the less new challenges or risk you will take. How will you know if you will or won't get your dream job if you never reach for it? If we never take risks, we can never learn what we might become or experience. Life is for living, look at your life and see if you have a good balance of security and challenge/risk taking.

89 "Love is never what you think it is"

Meditation: Love is whatever one thinks it to be. But on a deeper level, the purest understanding of it cannot be told in words. Every thought of what it is, is just that…a thought. But love can still be known by the thoughtless, felt by the armless and experienced by the inexperienced. For it's the immovable space from which existence flowers and blooms from.

90 "There are no real *Shoulds*, only *Coulds*"

Meditation: Life is about choice, we wouldn't enjoy life if we had no choice. In the ego-less understanding which is outside of the human experience, rules do not exist. When you get upset with someone, a friend or colleague for example, you are upset at them for not doing what *you* feel they should do. When looking from a larger perspective you find they don't have to, they could, but don't need too. Don't force frustration onto yourself by saying people should or should not do that, instead, if we wish to have more peace within, say one *could* do something. Suggest instead of order, the choice is yours.

91 "Fear loves me, fear wants to help me"

Meditation: Fear is needed in our physical forms. Don't ignore fear that arises within you, love fear. For it's because of fear that we know which belief systems are holding us back from freedom. Go inwards now, and meet the emotion of fear. Does this entity we call fear, have any real power over you? What can it do to you? Is it conscious? does it even exist?

92 "All levels of consciousness are available to me right now"

Meditation: Through your power of intention, you can choose to perceive the world as your ego, higher self (higher state of consciousness), or as pure awareness. The holy *trinity* has been conceptualised by many a person over many years. May this version of the *trinity* help you see that the *trinity* is you. Direct your intention towards each of these 3 states, marinate in their essence. Does the sense of them differ? If so, how do they all differ?

93 "Meditation is the front row seat to your thoughts"

Meditation: Meditation is not about attempting to not think, it's about being still enough to realise you are observing thoughts that don't belong to you. For if to you they did belong, they wouldn't appear without your say so.

94 "The bigger picture is bigger than the bigger picture"

Meditation: Some say looking at the bigger picture is a luxury that only the privileged who's future is secure can have. How can you say you don't have the luxury of looking at the bigger picture, when you don't yet know that which you are? You believe you are the person, a person can experience lack, but the person is only an accumulation of beliefs and knowledge.

Beliefs and knowledge is thought that is remembered. So, who are you when you're not attaching to floating thoughts such as memories? You only experience lack when you attach to the belief that you're the owner of these thoughts that appear and disappear claiming to be you. But they cannot be the essence of you since they come and go as they please. Who or what is the one that is aware of the feeling of lack? The real bigger picture is, you believe you are in the picture as an individual entity, but what you are is the observer of the whole picture.

95 "Pass your passion to the all"

Meditation: The answer to the question *what are you most passionate about?* should be "Life". In everything you do in life, you should do with your full attention. Passion is simply the strength of the attention you give to something that you enjoy. Why limit your passion to one thing? Are you passionate about life? Only the passionate can find truth.

96 "You are, me"

Meditation: Look behind the person you believe you are, remember a persona is a character. Who were we before we were given a persona? What you are is what I am, the undefinable space that holds this construct called "life", together.

97 "Incubate in the sense of nothingness"

Meditation: We say the word "Nothing" a lot in our everyday conversations. But what is nothing? No-thing? Or something more than this? Can it be felt, seen or heard? If nothing can exist? Isn't that a contradiction? If so, what's the truth of nothing-ness? Your mission right now is to seek out this nothing-ness and see what you sense/find there.

98 "When you close your eyes, you open the self"

Meditation: Are you simply an accumulation of your senses? Or do you use your senses? Do you exist without any of the 5 senses? Close your eyes and sit in stillness to look for this answer.

99 "The Universe is not inside of you, you are that"

Meditation: If the universe is inside of you, then *what* are you?

100 "Labels are for items, I am no item"

Meditation: Names are labels that can distract us from what we truly are. Names promote division and hierarchy. Do not be the one who is fooled into believing somebody is different to you just because of their name, always remember they acquired that name through another person's decision. Before given the name, they were (and still are) a variation of you. For they are you.

101 "Do it now, or never do it at all"

Meditation: There is only *now*. Only *now* exist. Everything else comes and goes. But now will always remain. There is only *now*. Only our mind makes things seem like *then,* but it's all *here* and all *now.* Plus, if one can say they possess a mind, then who or what is holding the mind in its possession? You see, you cannot be the mind. There is only *now*. Only different expressions of *now*. Where is *now*? It's in the stillness between the thought and emotion. The truth lives there. The understanding resides there. The being-ness lives there. There is only *now.* Where no movement exist. Nothing is needed. No balance or joy. No sadness or happiness. Just now-ness. Just truth. Just the potential for that which perceives, to do its perceiving. There is only *now,*

Be...here...*now.* Sit in the gap between your thoughts. Come home. Join the all. For you are me and I am you. The mind's projections are projecting onto something. So, what is that something? Discover this for yourself...

Other titles by the author include:

Mastering Communication – The 10 Keys to Unlocking Your Enlightened Voice

Thank You for Reading.

www.ingramcontent.com/pod-product-compliance
Lightning Source LLC
Chambersburg PA
CBHW031959040426
42448CB00006B/417